The Story of a Special Day
Volume 179

June
27

The 178th day of the year (179th in leap years). There are 187 days remaining until the end of the year.

by Michael Dobson

Timespinner
Press

This book is also available in e-book form for Kindle, e-pub devices, and other formats from your favorite online booksellers.

For more information about the series, about us, or about your special day, please email us at editor@timespinnerpress.com.

Look for other volumes in *The Story of a Special Day*, coming often. See www.timespinnerpress.com for details and for the most recent information.

Table of Contents

Quote of the Day

"The free expression of the hopes and aspirations of a people is the greatest and only safety in a sane society."

Emma Goldman, feminist and anarchist
born June 27, 1869

Today
in
History
THEMA
ACO
MAGNA
June 27

Martyrdom of Joseph and Hiram Smith in Carthage Jail, June 27, 1844, by G. W. Fasel and C. G. Crehen, circa 1851

The Battle of Kenesaw Mountain (Credit: Kurz & Allison, 1891)

What Happened on June 27?

From the creation of great works of engineering and art, to devastating wars and natural disasters, thousands of years of history have left their mark on each and every day of the year. Here are some additional important events that occurred on June 27. (Illustrated items are shaded.)

1844 — Founder of the Church of the Latter Day Saints **(Mormons) Joseph Smith and his brother Hyrum are killed by a mob** in Carthage, Illinois.

1864 — The American Civil War **Battle of Kennesaw Mountain** takes place during Sherman's march toward Atlanta.

1898 — Adventurer and sailor **Joshua Slocum** becomes the first man to complete a **solo circumnavigation** of the Earth. *(Photo next page)*

1905 — A rebellion breaks out aboard the Russian battleship *Potemkin*; chronicled in Sergei Eisenstein's 1925 silent film classic *The Battleship Potemkin*. *(Photo next page)*

1950 — The United States decides to enter the **Korean War**.

1971 — Rock impressario Bill Graham closes New York's **Fillmore East**, known as the "Church of Rock and Roll."

Joshua Slocum aboard his ship *Spray* in Sidney, 1896

Mobs burn the port of Odessa during the *Potemkin* mutiny, 1905

Quote of the Day

"We differ, blind and seeing, one from another, not in our senses, but in the use we make of them, in the imagination and courage with which we seek wisdom beyond the senses."

Helen Keller, writer and social activist
became deaf and blind from an illness in infancy
born June 27, 1880

Births
and
Deaths
THERI
ACA
MAGNA
June 27

Bob Keeshan, known to generations of children as "Captain Kangaroo," was born June 27, 1927

Notable June 27 People

With the current world population at about seven billion people, on average about 19 million people also celebrate their birthdays on June 27 — and that isn't counting the millions and millions who came before! No matter when you were born, you share your birthday with many special people whose accomplishments (and occasionally embarrassments) have been noted as part of history.

In this section, you'll meet fascinating people who share your birthday. They're organized by what they're famous for, and then in reverse chronological order from most recent to earliest. Those who are shown in photographs or artwork have a box around them. We don't have photos of everyone, so please forgive us if your favorite person is missing.

Some of these people you've heard of, others may be new to you, but they all make up an important part of the reason that June 27 is a truly special day!

An 8year old **Helen Keller** (left) with tutor Anne Sullivan,1888

Who Was Born on June 27?

Cover Story/Person of the Day
Helen Keller (1880)

Helen Keller is best known today for her portrayal in the play and film *The Miracle Worker*, depicting how a person both deaf and blind was able to learn to communicate with the help of her teacher and lifelong companion Anne Sullivan.

Born June 27, 1880, in Tuscumbia, Alabama, Helen Keller contracted an unknown illness at the age of 19 months that left her both deaf and blind. She was able to communicate somewhat by means of signs, and by the age of seven could single out individuals by the vibrations their footsteps made.

Her parents looked for ways to educate the young girl, and were eventually referred to inventor Alexander Graham Bell, who was working with deaf children. Through Bell, the parents met 20-year old Anne Sullivan, who was herself visually impaired, and hired her to instruct their daughter.

Sullivan taught Helen Keller to communicate by spelling words into her hand, and after a few frustrating months, Keller figured out the connection between the spelled-out word "water" and the sensation of water running over her hand.

An eager student, Helen Keller soon knew the names of many familiar objects. She learned to enjoy music by feeling the beat, and learned to talk. She could "hear" others by reading their lips with her hands.

She attended Radcliffe College, where she became the first deaf and blind student to earn a Bachelor's degree. Widely recognized for her intelligence and drive, she was admired by such people as Mark Twain.

A passionate advocate for people with disabilities as well as for other social causes, Helen Keller became a world-renowned speaker and author. A suffragist, a pacficist, and a radical socialist, she helped to found the American Civil Liberties Union. When establishment newspapers refused to print her views, she protested until they were forced to change their minds.

A major force in Helen Keller's radicalism was her discovery, by investigating conditions of the blind, that many cases were traceable to industrial conditions. She became a member of the Industrial Workers of the World ("Wobblies," see pg. 38) to fight for improved conditions. As her health diminished late in life, she spent her energies raising funds for the American Foundation for the Blind.

On June 1, 1968, a few weeks before her 88th birthday, Helen Keller died in her sleep at her home in Easton, Connecticut. She was cremated and her ashes were placed at the National Cathedral in Washington, DC, along with her companions Anne Sullivan and Polly Thompson.

Listed as one of the most widely admired people of the 20th century, she was awarded the Presidential Medal of Freedom and named to the National Women's Hall of Fame. Her life's story has been told in numerous books and films.

Helen Keller (left) with Mark Twain, 1895 (Courtesy Wellcome Images, CC BY-SA 4.0)

Illustration by **Kate Carew,** accompanying an interview with the
Wright Brothers (Credit: New York *World)*

More June 27 Birthdays

Art and Illustration

Kate Carew, known as the "only woman caricaturist" for her illustrated celebrity interviews for the New York *World. (1869)*

Business

Ross Perot, became a billionaire after founding Electronic Data Systems; ran an independent campaign for President in 1992 and 1996, receiving one of the strongest showing by a third party or independent candidate in US history. *(1930)*

Juan Trippe, aviation pioneer who founded Pan American World Airways. *(1899)*

Crime and Punishment

Konrad Kujau, German illustrator and forger who created the *Hitler Diaries,* which he sold for DM2.5 million, resulting in a 4.5-year prison sentence. *(1938)*

Fashion and Design

Vera Wang, fashion designer whose best known work includes wedding gowns and other clothes for such people as Chelsea Clinton, Ivanka Trump, Mariah Carey, and Sarah Michelle Gellar. *(1945)*

Norma Kamali, fashion designer best known for creating the bathing suit worn by Farrah Fawcett in her iconic 1976 poster. *(1949)*

Government

Charles Stewart Parnell, Irish nationalist politician who played a key role in the Home Rule movement that advocated Irish self-government. *(1846)*

Journalism and Literature

Alice McDermott, won the American Book Award and the US National Book Award for Fiction for her 1998 novel *Charming Billy*. *(1953)*

Peter Maas, jouranlist and author best known for his work related to crime, including *The Valachi Papers*, *Underboss*, and others. *(1929)*

Catherine Cookson, writer primarily of romance novels, at one time the best-selling author in Great Britain. *(1906)*

Lafcadio Hearn, writer best known for his books on Japan, bringing the culture and legends of that country to Western attention. Known in Japan as Koizumi Yakumo (小泉 八雲). *(1850)*

Military

Paul Mauser, German weapon designer and manufacturer who created the Mauser line of rifles and pistols, used extensively by the German military. *(1838)*

Lafcadio Hearn (left) with wife Koizumi Setsu

Music

Lorrie Morgan, country music singer whose number one hits include "Five Minutes," "What Part of No," and "I Didn't Know My Own Strength." *(1959)*

Joey Covington, rock drummer who played with Jefferson Airplane/Starship and Hot Tuna. *(1945)*

Bruce Johnson, singer-songwriter and producer best known as a member of The Beach Boys and for writing the 1975 Barry Manilow hit "I Write the Songs." *(1942)*

Doc Pomus, blues singer-songwriter inducted into the Rock and Roll Hall of Fame, the Songwriters Hall of Fame, and the Blues Hall of Fame. He co-wrote such hits as "A Teenager in Love," "Save the Last Dance for Me," and "This Magic Moment." *(1913)*

George Walker, African-American composer who was the first to win the Pulitzer Prize for Music for his work *Lilacs. (1922)*

Elton Britt, country music guitarist and singer-songwriter best known for his wartime hit, "There's a Star-Spangled Banner Waving Somewhere." *(1913)*

Elton Britt

Performing Arts

Khloé Kardashian, socialite and television personality best known for starring along with her family in the reality series *Keeping Up with the Kardashians* and its spinoffs. *(1984)*

Tobey Maguire, actor best-known for portraying the title character in the Sam Raimi *Spider-Man* trilogy as well as for his roles in such films as *Seabiscuit, The Good German,* and *The Great Gatsby. (1975)*

Christian Kane, actor best known as Lindsey MacDonald on *Angel* and Eliot Spencer on *Leverage. (1972)*

Jo Frost, best known for her work on the reality television series *Supernanny* and for writing several books on child care. *(1971)*

J. J. Abrams, filmmaker whose work includes the television series *Lost* and *Fringe,* and films *Star Trek* (2009) and *Star Wars: The Force Awakens* (2015). *(1966)*

Isabelle Adjani, French actresss who is the only person to win the César Award five times; nominated twice for the Academy Award for Best Actress for *The Story of Adele H.* (1975) and *Camille Claudel* (1988). *(1955)*

Julia Duffy, actress best known as Stephanie on the 1980s sitcom *Newhart. (1951)*

Bob Keeshan, television actor and producer best known for creating and playing the title role in the children's television show *Captain Kangaroo*, which ran from 1955 to 1984. Also played the original Clarabell the Clown on the *Howdy Doody Show.* *(1927) (Photo page 8.)*

John McIntire, American character actor who appeared in 65 films and numerous TV series; best known for his role on *Wagon Train. (1907)*

John McIntire on *Wagon Train*

Antoinette "Tony" Perry, Broadway actress and director who is best remembered as the namesake of the Tony Awards for theatrical performance. *(1888)*

Antoinette "Tony" Perry (Photo: Theodore C. Marceau

May Irwin, vaudeville star best known for performing the first on-screen kiss in the 1896 Thomas Edison Kinetoscope film *The Kiss. (1862) (Photo next page)*

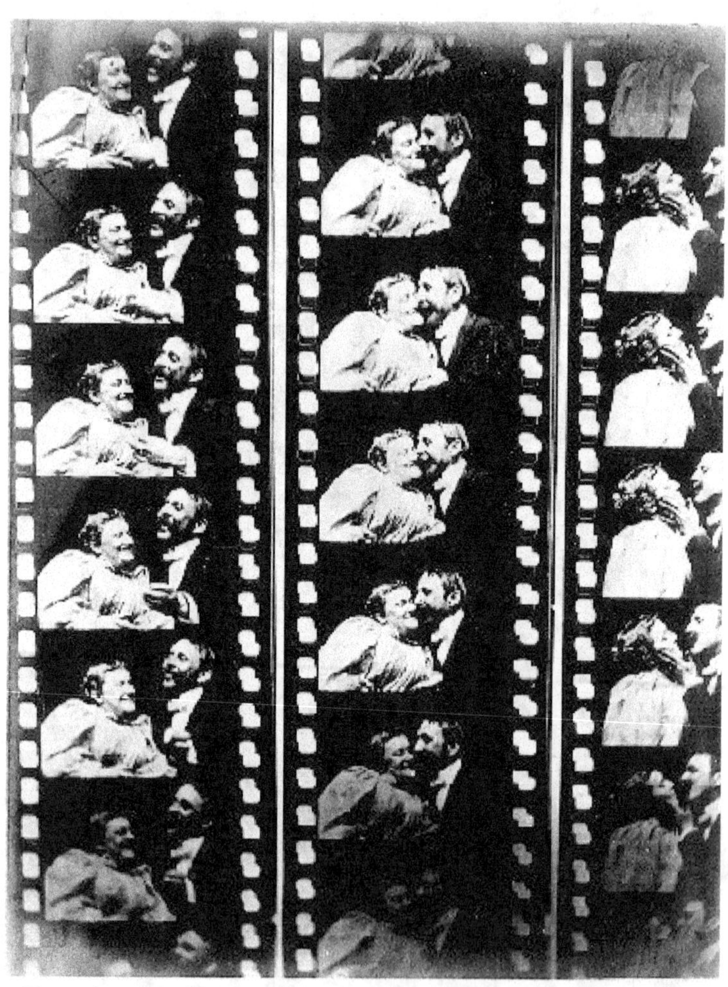

From the 1896 Thomas Edison film *The Kiss*, starring **May Irwin**
(Courtesy Thomas Edison National Historic Site)

Science

Martinus J. G. Veltman, Dutch scientist who shared the 1999 Nobel Prize in Physics for his work on particle theory. *(1931)*

Hans Spemann, German embryologist awarded the 1935 Nobel Prize in Physiology or Medicine for his discovery of the mechanism by which the embryo directed the development of groups of cells into specific tissues and organs. *(1869)*

Social Activism

Emma Goldman, Anarchist political activist and writer sometimes called "the most dangerous woman in America," known for her advocacy of women's rights and other causes; imprisoned several times for "inciting to riot" for illegally distributing information about birth control. An initial supporter of the Bolshevik revolution, she became disillusioned and denounced the revolution for its suppresion of dissent. *(1869*)* *(Photo next page)*

---

* Emma Goldman was born in the Russian Empire in 1869, which did not convert to the modern Gregorian calendar until 1918. She moved to the United States in 1885 and lived in the US and Canada until her death in 1940. Her birthdate on the "Old Style" Julian calendar was June 15, 1869, which was the same day as June 27 on the "New Style" Gregorian calendar, so both days are usually given for her date of birth. For more about the different types of calendars, see "What Day of the Week is June 27?"

Emma Goldman (Photo: T. Kajiwara)

Sports

Viktor Petrenko (Віктор Петренко), won the 1992 Olympic gold medal in men's singles figure skating, representing Ukraine. *(1969)*

Sylvie Fréchette, won the 1992 Olympic gold medal for women's solo synchronized swimming. *(1967)*

Dick the Bruiser, real name William Afflis; played for the Green Bay Packers before starting a professional wrestling career as Dick the Bruiser, "the World's Most Dangerous Wrestler," a title that inspired David Letterman's "Worlds's Most Dangerous Band." *(1929)*

Adolf Kiefer, American swimmer who received a gold medal in the 1936 Summer Olympics; first person to swim the 100-yard backstroke in under a minute. *(1918)*

Willie Mosconi, professional pool player who won the World Straight Pool Championship 15 times and is credited for helping popularize pool; among the first inductees to the Billiard Congress of America Hall of Fame. *(1913)*

Wanda Gág

Who Died on June 27?

Art and Illustration

Tove Jansson, novelist and illustrator best known for the *Moomin* books. *(2001)*

Wanda Gág, wrote and illustrated the children's classics *Millions of Cats* and *The ABC Bunny. (1946)*

Government

Milada Horáková, Czech politician convicted and executed by the Communist government for conspiracy and treason; subsequently cleared of all charges following the Velvet Revolution that ended Communist rule in that country. *(1950)*

Maharaja Ranjit Singh, known as Sher-i-Punjab ("Lion of the Punjab"), who united the Sikhs in western India and built the Sikh Empire, which fell apart after his death. *(1839) (Photo next page.)*

Journalism and Literature

Shelby Foote, award-winning historian and novelist best known to the public for his appearance in the 1990 Ken Burns PBS documentary *The Civil War. (2005)*

Maharaja Ranjit Singh

Military

George Patton IV, US Army major general and son of the World War II general George S. Patton, Jr.. *(2004)*

Music

Chris Squire, singer-songwriter and bass guitarist best known as a founding member of the rock band Yes, member of the Rock and Roll Hall of Fame. *(2015)*

John Entwistle, original bass guitarist for The Who, member of the Rock and Role Hall of Fame. *(2002)*

John Entwistle (Credit: Jean-Luc, CC BY-SA 2.0)

Performing Arts

Corey Allen, actor and filmmaker best known as Buzz Gunderson in the 1955 film *Rebel Without a Cause. (2010)*

Gale Storm, actress known for her roles on the 1950s television shows *My Little Margie* and *The Gale Storm Show. (2009)*

Joan Sims, English actress best known for the *Carry On* films. *(2001)*

Jack Lemmon, eight-time Academy Award nominee with two wins; famous for such films as *Some Like It Hot, The Apartment, Mister Roberts, Days of Wine and Roses, The Great Race,* and the *Odd Couple. (2001)*

Albert "Cubby" Broccoli, film producer most notably for the *James Bond* franchise. *(1996)*

Religion

Joseph Smith, claimed to have discovered the golden plates on which were inscribed *The Book of Mormon;* founder of the Church of Jesus Christ of Latter Day Saints. Established a Mormon settlement in Illinois, where he was arrested and killed along with his brother **Hyrum Smith** by a mob that stormed the jailhouse. *(1844) (Photo page 2.)*

Trailer for the 1959 film *Some Like It Hot.* From left to right: Tony Curtis, **Jack Lemmon,** and Marilyn Monroe

Science

James Smithson, English chemist and mineralogist who left his fortune to the United States "to found in Washington, under the name of the Smithsonian Institution, an establishment for the increase and diffusion of knowledge among men." *(1829)*

The Smithsonian Institution "Castle," Washington, DC, resting place of **James Smithson** (Courtesy Wellcome Images)

Sports

Daniel Kinsey, won a gold medal in hurdling at the 1924 Paris Olympic Games. *(1970)*

Lottie Dod, English sportswoman who won at Wimbledon five times; also competed in golf, field hocky, and archery. Won a silver medal in archery at the 1908 Olympic Games. Cited in *The Guinness Book of Records* as the most versatile female athlete of all time (tied with Babe Zaharias). *(1960)*

Lottie Dod

Quote of the Day

"One of the big secrets of finding time is
not to watch television."

Bob Keeshan, "Captain Kangaroo"
born June 27, 1927

Holidays
Around
the World

June 27

The Seven Sleepers of Ephesus, by Menologion of Basil (c. 985 CE) — for **SIEBENSCHLÄFERTAG,** celebrated June 27

June 27 Holidays and Celebrations

If you're looking for a reason to take your special day off, you should know that every single day is a holiday somewhere in the world! Here's some of what you can celebrate on June 27!

General Events

Siebenschläfertag (German-speaking nations)
In the legend of the Seven Sleepers of Ephesus, common to Christian and Islamic traditions and dating back before 500 CE, a group of young people hide in a cave near Ephesus to escape religious prosecution, and emerge 300 years later.

In German popular traditions, the weather conditions on Seven Sleepers Day, June 27, predict the summer weather of the next seven weeks, similar to the US Groundhog Day.

Canadian Multiculturalism Day
Canada demonstrates its commitment to multiculturalism and raises awareness of the topic each year on June 27.

Commemoration Day for Victims of the Communist Regime (Czech Republic)
The Czech Republic honors those who suffered under Communist rule on the anniversary of the execution of Milada Horáková, June 27, 1950. *(See page 27.)*

Dia do Mestiço (Brazil)

Brazil celebrates all its mixed-race people on June 27. It is an official public holiday in the states of Amazonas, Roraima, Mato Grosso, and Paraíba.

Day of Turkmen Workers of Culture and Art (Turkmenistan)

The nation of Turkmenistan honors those who work in culture and the arts as a public holiday on June 27.

Independence Day (Djibouti)

The African nation of Djibouti celebrates its independence from France on June 27, 1977, with a national public holiday.

Industrial Workers of the World Day (international)

The IWW labor union (sometimes called the "Wobblies") was founded June 27, 1905, with the goal of promoting worker solidarity. While it is a relatively small organization today, at its height it had more than 150,000 members and was a major force in the early labor union movement.

National HIV Testing Day (United States)

The US Department of Health and Human Services promotes awareness of the role of HIV testing in containing the spread of AIDS.

National PTSD Awareness Day (United States)
Established by the US Senate in 2010, this day is dedicated to creating awareness of post-traumatic stress disorder. The entire month of June is designated as PTSD Awareness Month.

Unity Day (Tajikistan)
Tajikistan celebrates National Unity Day on June 27.

An Industrial Workers of the World "stickerette," circa 1919 — for
INDUSTRIAL WORKERS OF THE WORLD DAY

Religious Feast Days and Holidays

Saint Days

Each day in the year is considered a feast day for one or more saints. They are somewhat different in western Christianity (Catholicism and many forms of Protestantism) and in eastern (Orthodox) Christianity. There are many others; this is a selection.

In *Western Christianity*, June 27 is the feast day of Saints Crescens, Cyril of Alexandria, and Ladislaus I of Hungary.

In *Eastern Orthodox Christianity*, it is also the commemoration of Saints Severus of Interocrea, Joanna the Myrrh-Bearer, and Luke the Hermit. (These saints are honored on June 14 by "Old Calendrists.[†]")

Moveable and Multi-Day Events

Some events take place over a specific week or time period. Start and finish dates may vary from year to year. Some events occur on different days each year (such as "fourth Saturday of a month"). These events sometimes take place on or include June 27.

Friday following the Third Sunday

- Take Your Dog to Work Day (United Kingdom)

[†] "Old Calendrists" use the older Julian calendar rather than the modern Gregorian calendar for liturgical purposes. June 14 on the Julian calendar is the same day as June 27 on the Gregorian calendar. For more about the different types of calendars, see "What Day of the Week is June 27?"

Last Thursday

- National Bomb Pop Day (United States)

Last Saturday

- Armed Forces Day (United Kingdom)
- Inventors' and Rationalizers' Day (Russia)
- Veterans Day (Netherlands)

Last Sunday

- Father's Day (Haiti)
- Log Cabin Day (Michigan, US)
- Mother's Day (Kenya)

Monday nearest to June 24

- Discovery Day (Newfoundland and Labrador)

Last Full Weekend

- Water Ski Days (US)

Two dogs in a bookshop, by Dirck and Salomon de Bray, 17th century — for TAKE YOUR DOG TO WORK DAY

Celebrations About Food

In the United States, almost every day of the year is dedicated to a particular food — some days honor more than one!. Sponsored by manufacturers, retailers, farmers, or simply fans, these days are often proclaimed by the President, Congress, state governors, or mayors.

In the US, June 27 is **National Orange Blossom Day.** Orange blossoms are the flowers of the orange tree, the state flower of Florida, and traditionally associated with good fortune.

Orange blossom water is used in French and Middle Eastern cuisine, primarily in desserts and baked goods. In Spain, orange blossoms are used to make tea. In the US, orange blossom water is used to make scones and marshmallows.

It is also thought by some to be an aphrodisiac.

The whole month of June is set aside to honorthe following foods.

- Georgia Blueberry Month
- National Candy Month
- National Dairy Month
- National Fresh Fruit and Vegetables Month
- National Iced Tea Month
- National Papaya Month

If June 27 falls on the last weekend of the month, it's also part of **North American Organic Brewers Days** and **Watermelon Seed Spitting Week**.

Orange Blossom, by Mary E. Eaton — for **NATIONAL ORANGE BLOSSOM DAY**

Sarah Vaughan, by William P. Gottlieb — for **AFRICAN-AMERICAN MUSIC APPRECIATION MONTH**

Honorary Months

Presidents, Congresses, and nations around the world issue proclamations recognizing particular months to honor certain causes. These events generally fall in April, though honorary months do come and go.

Holidays established by states and nonprofit organizations are listed if verified. If not otherwise specified, all months are US. There is some variation from year to year; some celebratory months get added and others get dropped. Two places to get up to date information are the current edition of Chase's Calendar of Events *or the website Brownielocks. Here are some honorary designations for June.*

- Adopt-a-Cat Month
- African-American Music Appreciation Month
- Caribbean American Heritage Month
- Children's Awareness Month
- Crop over (Barbados), celebrated until the first Monday in August.
- Dairy Alternative Month
- Fireworks Safety Month
- Gay and Lesbian Pride Month (US)
- Great Outdoors Month (US)
- International Surf Music Month
- Men's Health Education and Awareness Month
- National Accordion Awareness Month
- National Camping Month

- National Rivers Month
- National Safety Month
- National Smile Month (UK)
- National Oceans Month (United States)
- PTSD Awareness Month
- Season of Emancipation (April 14 to August 23) (Barbados)
- Women's Golf Month
- World Naked Bike Ride Month (northern hemisphere)

Just for Fun

Anybody can make up a holiday, and many people do! While none of these are officially recognized and some may come and go, here are a few more holidays for June 27.

- Please Take My Children to Work Day (last Monday)
- National Sunglasses Day

A child preparing for police duty at US Customs and Border Patrol
— for **PLEASE TAKE MY CHILDREN TO WORK DAY**

Quote of the Day

"Do you recall that night in June
Upon the Danube River;
We listened to the ländler-tune,
We watched the moonbeams quiver."

— Charles A. Aïdé, "Danube River"

49

June, by Eugène Grasset

June: The Sixth Month

And what is so rare as a day in June?
Then, if ever, come perfect days;
Then Heaven tries earth if it be in tune,
And over it softly her warm ear lays.

— *James Russell Lowell*

In the Julian and Gregorian calendars, June is the sixth month of the year. It's one of the four months that have only 30 days. No months start on the same day of the week as June, an oddity shared only by May. However, June ends on the same day of the week as March in both common and leap years.

In the Northern Hemisphere, June is the month with the longest daylight hours; in the Southern Hemisphere, it's the one with the shortest, equivalent to December. The meteorological summer begins June 21 (the Summer Solstice) in the Northern Hemisphere; the meteorological winter begins on the same day in the Southern Hemisphere (the Winter Solstice).

The English name of June takes its name from the Latin *Iunius*. The poet Ovid gives two theories for the origin of the name. The first is that June is named for the Roman goddess Juno, wife of Jupiter and queen of the gods. The second is that the name comes from the Latin word *iuniores* ("younger ones"), and that the previous month of May comes from *maiores* ("elders")

As the early Roman calendar started its new year in March, June was originally the fourth month of the year. It's uncertain when the Romans switched the new year to January, but it may have been as late as 153 BCE.

June, George Auriol

June in Other Cultures

The month of June has different names in different languages. Some nations use calendars other than the Gregorian, and their months may overlap with June. In lunar-based calendars, such as Islam, months move through the seasons, but they often have a word for June itself.

Albanian: Qershor
Arabic (Egyptian, Sudanese, Moroccan): يونيو (*yūniyū*)
Arabic (Levantine): حزيران (*ḥuzayrān*)
Arabic (Libyan): الصيف (*al-sayf*)
Arabic (Algerian): جوان (*Juwān*)
Azerbaijani: İyun
Basque: Ekain

Bulgarian: юни (*juni*)

Chinese: 六月 (Cantonese: *luhkyuht*; Mandarin: *liùyuè*; Taiwanese: *lak-goeh*)

Corsican: Chjugnu

Czech: červen

Finnish: Kesäkuu

French: Juin

German, Norwegian: Juni

Greek: Ιούνιος (*Ioúnios*)

Hebrew: יוני (*yûnî*)

Hindi: जून (*jūn*)

Hungarian: Június

Irish (Gaelic): Meitheamh mí an Mheithimh

Italian: Giugno

Japanese (traditional calendar): 六月 (*rokugatsu*); 水無月 (*minaduki*)

Korean: 유월 (*yuweol*)

Lithuanian: Birželis

Maori: Pipiri

Old English: Sēremōnaþ

Polish: Czerwiec

Russian: июнь (*ijun'*)

Sesotho: Phupjane

Spanish: Junio

Swedish, Swahili: Juni

Thai: Mithunayon

Vietnamese: 腈趶 (tháng sáu)

Welsh: Mehefin

June Brides (and Other Sayings and Superstitions)

June is the most popular month for weddings, followed by August. There are a number of sayings and superstitions about June brides and June weddings.

"A June bride is joyful, jubilant, and jolly well jovial."

"A June bride will be impetuous, and generous."

"Married in the month of roses (June), life will be one long honeymoon."

"Marry when June roses grow, over land and sea you'll go."

"When you marry in June, you'll be a bride all your life." (from the song *June Bride*.)

Which day to get married? That's easy. "Monday for wealth, Tuesday for health, Wednesday the best day of all, Thursday for losses, Friday for crosses, Saturday for no luck at all."

Why such an emphasis on June? Some say it's in honor of Juno, the goddess of marriage. Others suggest it's because back in Medieval days, people would usually have their (yes) annual bath in May, so they'd still be relatively fresh by June. This may also explain the custom of the bridal bouquet.

According to superstition, May is the most unlucky month for marriages, but in ancient Rome the "inauspicious" period ran from May 15 to June 15. The high priestess of Jupiter told the poet Ovid to delay his daughter's wedding until after that date.

There are also some June proverbs for farmers.

"A calm June puts the farmer in tune."

"June damp and warm, does the farmer no harm."

June Symbols

Birthstone Pearl, moonstone, or alexandrite.

Pearl

Moonstone

Alexandrite

Birth Flowers Rose and Honeysuckle

Roses, by Vincent van Gogh

Honeysuckle

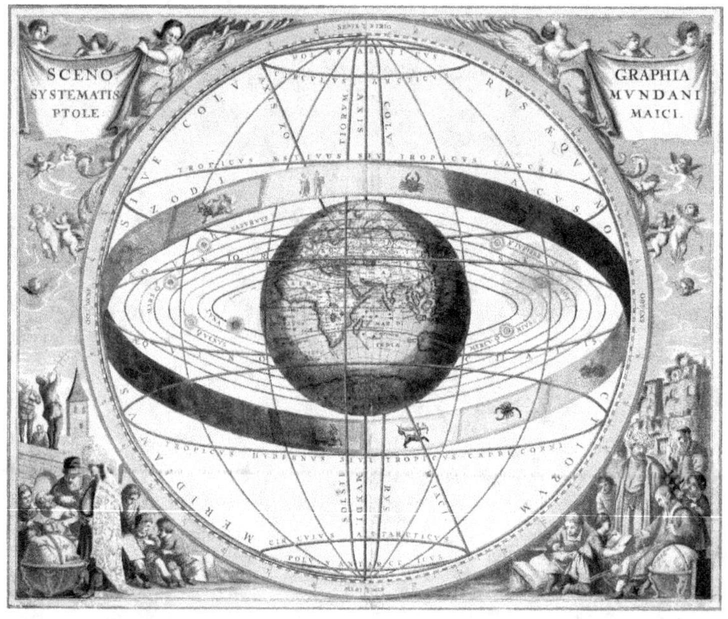

Scenography of the Ptolemaic Cosmography, by Johannes van Loon, based on Andreas Cellarius's *Harmonia Macrocosmica,* 1660

June 27 Zodiac Signs

From the perspective of someone on Earth, the Sun appears to move through the sky throughout the year, along a path astronomers call the *ecliptic plane*. The ecliptic plane is divided into twelve constellations, known as the zodiac, based on traditionally observed patterns of stars. On your birthday, you can't see your constellation, because it's in the daytime sky.

The zodiac was first developed by Babylonian astronomers about 2,500 years ago. Because they were unaware that the Earth wobbles like a spinning top (known as *precession*), they didn't make allowance for the fact that the Sun's path through the zodiac changes over time.

That means there are now two sets of dates for your birth sign. The *tropical dates* are the original Babylonian dates; the *sidereal dates* tell you where the Sun actually appears as it moves along its annual path.

For June 27, the tropical sign is **Cancer** and the sidereal sign is **Gemini.**

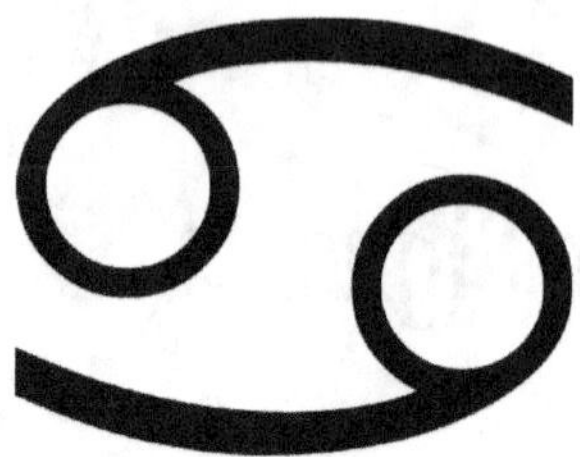

Cancer

Tropical June 21 to July 22
Sidereal July 16 to August 15

The Greek word for "crab" is Καϱκινος (Karkinos), later Latinized as *carcinus*, which evolved into our word *cancer*. In Greek mythology. In one telling, when Hercules was battling the Hydra, Zeus's wife Hera sent Karkinos to distract the hero, but Hercules kicked it with such force that it was thrown into the sky, becoming a constellation. (Some say that Hercules crushed the crab with his foot and that Hera placed the crab in the night sky as a reward for its service.)

Because of the association with the disease, some astrologers refer to those born under the sign of Cancer as "moon children," because the ruling planet of Cancer is the Moon.

Cancers (or Moon Children) are supposed to be loyal, dependable, caring, and adaptable, but can also be moody, self-pitying, and oversensitive. Cancers are supposed to be particularly compatible with Scorpios, Piceans, and other Cancers.

Gemini

Tropical May 22 to June 21
Sidereal June 16 to July 15

According to Greek mythology, Leda, wife of the King of Sparta, gave birth to Helen of Troy and Clytemnestra. The god Zeus, disguised as a swan, seduced her after she had already lain with her husband on the same night. This resulted in two eggs, which hatched to become the twins Castor and Pollux. Castor's father was the King of Sparta, but Pollux was the son of Zeus and therefore immortal. When Castor died, Pollux shared his immortality, so that they could divide their time between Hades and Olympus. They were enshrined in the Zodiac as the constellation Gemini, the Twins.

In astrology, Gemini is an air sign, ruled by Mercury, compatible with Libra, Aquarius, and Aries. Geminis are supposed to be communicative, flexible, intellectual, and curious, but prone to fickleness and easily distracted.

Illustration by Edward Penfield

What Day of the Week is June 27?

On what day of the week does June 27 fall?

Surprisingly, this isn't an easy question. Because the calendar year is 365 days long (366 in leap years), it doesn't divide evenly by the seven days of the week.

Also, the Earth goes around the Sun in about 365-1/4 days, so a calendar tends to drift over time. That's why the same date falls on different weekdays in different years.

This is made even more complicated by a change in calendars that took place in 1582. Our modern calendar has its roots in ancient Rome, in a calendar reform conducted by Julius Caesar. Caesar commissioned mathematicians to attack the problem, and they came up with the idea of leap years, and thus standardized the calendar for centuries to come. This was called the Julian calendar.

Over time, however, the small errors in Caesar's calculation compounded. That's why Pope Gregory XIII commissioned the Gregorian calendar, used in most of the world today. Some countries converted in 1582, when the calendar was first developed; some converted later; other still haven't changed.

Gregorian and Julian aren't the only types of calendars. The Hebrew year, the Islamic year, and many other calendars are used in different parts of the world and among different people.

You can convert Gregorian dates to other calendars, including the Hebrew calendar, the Islamic calendar, and even the Mayan calendar by visiting the Fourmilab Calendar Converter at http://www.fourmilab.ch/documents/calendar/.

Chinese calendar systems are quite complex and have changed several times; a full discussion is far beyond the scope of this book. If you're interested, you can find information here: http://www.hermetic.ch/cal_stud/chinese_cal.htm.

On Names and Dates

Historians use "CE" (Common Era) and "BCE" (Before the Common Era) instead of the more common "AD" (Anno Domini, or Year of Our Lord) and "BC" (Before Christ), reflecting the fact that the year-numbering system established by the Gregorian calendar is used throughout the world in many countries not culturally Christian.

The CE/BCE designation dates back to at least 1708, and has been adopted as a standard by the United Nations and the Universal Postal Union. Because this series of books covers events and people of all nations and cultures, we use the CE/BCE terms.

The abbreviation "O.S." ("Old Style") and "N.S." ("New Style") on some dates refers to the fact that the Russian Empire (in particular) did not switch from the Julian to the Gregorian calendar at the same time as the rest of Europe, and therefore some figures and events have two dates.

Also, in the Julian calendar in England in the 16th century, the year began on March 25 rather than January 1. To avoid confusion with Gregorian dates, dates between January and March were often written using both years.

People and events whose original names are not in the Western alphabet have their native names (where possible) in the appropriate script shown in parenthesis. If you are using an e-reader to access an electronic version of this book, all characters don't always display on all devices.

A 50-year brass perpetual calendar.

Quote of the Day

"Time is an illusion, lunchtime doubly so."

Douglas Adams,
from *The Hitchhiker's Guide to the Galaxy*

Notes and Credits
Timespinner Press

Cartoon by John T. McCutcheon

Copyright, Credit, and Contact

Follow Us

Our blog "This Day in History" (http://
timespinnerpress.com/this-day-in-history/) features short
articles on events and people associated with each day, and
updates several times each week. Also subscribe to the
"Quote of the Day" at http://timespinnerpress.com/quote-
of-the-day/. You can get daily links by following us on
Facebook at TimespinnerPress, or on Twitter as
@sidewisethinker.

Contact Us

Find an error or a format problem? Want information about
the series, about us, or about when the volume for your
special day might be available? Please email us at
editor@timespinnerpress.com. (We also take requests if your
special day isn't yet complete. Please give us at least six
weeks' notice if possible.)

Sources

We owe a great debt to Wikipedia, which is our first stop for
research. We attempt to make independent confirmation of
all important dates and facts through a variety of other
sources.

Other sources we frequently use include the Library of
Congress; "on this day" listings from *Encyclopedia Britannica*,
the *New York Times*, and the BBC; Omniglot for the names of
months in other languages; *Chase's Calendar of Events*; and, of
course, the always essential Google.

All art and photographs are either in the public domain, used under a Creative Commons license, or with a "fair use" justification, and most frequently come from Wikimedia Commons and the Library of Congress Prints and Photographs Division.

Attribution is provided where possible, or as requested by the copyright owner, or when there is particular historical significance, listed below. For information about any particular illustration or photograph, please contact us.

Credits

1. The 1904 portrait photograph of Helen Keller used on the cover is in the public domain because its copyright has expired. The photographer is unknown. The image is from the collection of the Library of Congress Prints and Photographs Division, digital ID cph.3c12513.

2. The illustration of the month of June used on the back cover is from the French Gothic illuminated manuscript *Les Très Riches Heures du duc de Berry* by the Limbourg Brothers, Jean Colombe, and an intermediate painter whose name is lost to history. It is in the public domain because its copyright has expired.

3. The box graphic used on the first page is from a 1916 pamphlet entitled "Divorce versus Democracy" authored by G. K. Chesterton, originally published in London by the Society of St. Peter and St. Paul. It is in the public domain in the US because it was published prior to 1923, and is in the public domain in all countries (including the country of origin) in which the copyright time is the author's life plus 70 years or less.

4. The graphic design for the section pages in this book is from a design originally created for a pharmacy label. It is courtesy of Wellcome Images (ICV No 11073, photo V0010813), and is used here under CC BY-SA 4.0.

5. The lithograph "Martyrdom of Joseph and Hiram *(sic)* Smith in Carthage Jail, June 27th, 1844. was painted by G. W. Fasel and lithographed by C. G. Crehen for Nagel & Weingaertner

was created circa 1851, and is in the public domain because its copyright has expired.

6. The painting "The Battle of Kenesaw *(sic)* Mountain," published by Kurz & Allison, was created circa 1891, and is in the public domain because its copyright has expired. It is from the collection of the Library of Congress, identifier LC-DIG-pga-01850.

7. The 1896 photograph of Joshua Slogan's ship *Spray* in Sydney Harbor is in the public domain because its copyright has expired. It is from the collection of the Australian National Maritime Museum, object 00002617. It has been cropped.

8. The 1905 photograph of the the Odessa port being burned by a mob during the *Potemkin* mutiny is in the public domain in Russia according to article 1256 of Book IV of the Civil Code of the Russian Federation No. 230-FZ of December 18, 2006. It is in the public domain in the US because it was published prior to January 1, 1923. It has been cropped.

9. The 1977 CBS publicity photograph of Bob Keeshan as "Captain Kangaroo" is in the public domain because it was published in the United States between 1923 and 1977 without a copyright notice. Traditionally, publicity photographs are not copyrighted because of the way in which they are intended to be used.

10. The 1888 photograph of Helen Keller (age 8) with her tutor Anne Sullivan on vacation in Cape Cod, Massachusetts, is in the public domain because its copyright has expired. It is in the collection of the New England Historic Geneaological Society.

11. The photograph of Helen Keller and Mark Twain was taken circa 1895, and is in the public domain because its copyright has expired. The file is courtesy of Wellcome Images, Photo M0018417, used here under CC BY-SA 4.0.

12. The illustration by Kate Carew was first published in the New York *World* prior to January 1, 1923, and is therefore in the public domain because its copyright has expired.

13. The photograph of Lafcadio Hearn and his wife was created prior to 1905 and is in the public domain because its copyright has expired.

14. The 1950 publicity photograph of Elton Britt is in the public domain because it was published in the United States between 1923 and 1977 without a copyright notice.

15. The 1961 publicity photograph of John McIntire from *Wagon Train* is in the public domain because it was published in the United States between 1923 and 1977 without a copyright notice.

16. The photograph of Antoinette Perry was taken circa 1910 by Theodore C. Marceau. It is in the public domain because its copyright has expired.

17. The filmstrip from the 1896 film *The Kiss* is in the public domain because its copyright has expired. It is courtesy Thomas Edison National Historical Site, National Park Service.

18. The photograph of Emma Goldman was taken circa 1910 by T. Kajiwara. It is in the public domain because its copyright has expired.

19. The 1916 photograph of Wanda Gág is in the public domain because its copyright has expired.

20. The painting of Maharaja Ranjit Singh was painted prior to 1839 and is in the public domain because its copyright has expired. The artist is unknown.

21. The 1980 photograph of John Entwistle in concert at MLG Toronto was taken by Jean-Luc, and is used here under CC BY-SA 2.0.

22. The 1959 screenshot from the trailer for *Some Like It Hot* is in the public domain because it was published in the United States between 1923 and 1977 without a copyright notice. Although the film is copyrighted, trailers were not generally copyrighted because of the way in which they are intended to be used. The image has been cropped.

23. The 19th century steel engraving of the Smithsonian Institution "castle" is by R. Metzeroth. It is in the public domain because its copyight has expired. The image file is courtesy Wellcome Images, photo V0014025, and is used here under CC BY-SA 4.0. The border has been cropped.

24. The 1891 photograph of Lottie Dod is in the public domain because its copyright has expired. The photographer is unknown.

25. The painting of the Seven Sleepers of Ephesus by Menologion of Basil was created circa 985 CE, and is in the public domain because its copyright has expired.

26. The Industrial Workers of the World "stickerette" was created circa 1919. It is in the public domain because it was published in the United States between 1923 and 1977 without a copyright notice. It is from the University of Washington Libraries Special Collections, accession number 0155-001.

27. The drawing "People and Two Dogs in a Book Shop" was created by either Dirck and/or Salomon de Bray between 1607 and 1678, and is in the public domain because its copyright has expired. It is from the collection of the Rijksmuseum Amsterdam, RP-T-1884-A-290.

28. The painting of an orange blossom by Mary E. Eaton appeared in *National Geographic* magazine in June 1917. It is in the public domain because its copyright has expired.

29. The 1946 photograph of Sarah Vaughan was taken by William P. Gottlieb, and is part of the William P. Gottlieb Collection of jazz photographs at the Library of Congress. In accordance with the wishes of Gottlieb, the photographs in the collection entered into the public domain in 2010.

30. The 2016 photograph of a child wearing police gear at US Customs and Border Protection headquarters, Washington, DC, is in the public domain as a work created by an employee of the US government as part of that person's official duties.

31. The 1896 drawing "June" by Eugène Grasset is in the public domain because its copyright has expired.

32. The 1912 graphic of June by George Auriol is in the public domain because its copyright has expired.

33. The 1815 woodcut of a proposal is in the public domain because its copyright has expired.

34. The photo of a pearl necklace is by "Anna reg," taken from Wikimedia Commons and used here under CC BY-SA 3.0.

35. The photograph of a Brazilian moonstone is by Didier Descouens, taken from Wikimedia Commons and used here under CC BY-SA 4.0.

36. The photograph of alexandrite under ultraviolet light is by
    Parent Géry, taken from Wikimedia Commons and used here
    because the creator has dedicated the rights to the public
    domain under CC0 1.0.

37. The painting *Roses* by Vincent Van Gogh can be found in the
    collection of the National Gallery of Art, Washington, DC.
    The image is in the public domain because its copyright has
    expired.

38. The illustration of honeysuckle originally appeared in the
    book *American Homes and Gardens*, published by Munn &
    Co., New York, in 1905. It is in the public domain because its
    copyright has expired. The image was taken from Flickr's
    The Commons.

39. The celestial sphere is from *Scenography of the Ptolemaic
    Cosmography*, by Johannes van Loon, based on Andreas
    Cellarius's *Harmonia Macrocosmica*, 1660. It is in the public
    domain because its copyright has expired.

40. The 1906 automobile calendar is by Edward Penfield, and is
    in the collection of the Library of Congress Prints and
    Photographs Division. It is in the public domain because its
    copyright has expired.

41. The 50-year perpetual calendar photograph is in the public
    domain.

42. The cartoon by John T. McCutcheon is from his 1905
    collection *The Mysterious Stranger and Other Cartoons by John
    T. McCutcheon*. It is in the public domain because its
    copyright has expired.

43. The painting "June" by Simon Bening is from the *Brevarium
    Grimani*, circa 1510, and is in the public domain because its
    copyright has expired.

44. The painting "June" by Hans Thoma is from his book
    Festkalender. It is in the public domain because it was
    published prior to 1923 and its copyright has expired.

License Description and Terms

Aside from material purely in the public domain, photographs and other material in this book are used under specific licenses permitting free use, usually with an attribution requirement. For full text and terms of these licenses, click or enter the appropriate links below. If you believe there is an error in the copyright status or attribution of any of these images, please email us.

- Creative Commons Attribution 2.0 Generic (CC-BY 2.0): http://creativecommons.org/licenses/by/2.0/deed.en
- Creative Commons Attribution-Share Alike 3.0 Generic (CC-BY-SA 3.0): http://creativecommons.org/licenses/by-sa/3.0/
- Creative Commons Attribution-Share Alike 2.5 Generic (CC-BY-SA 2.5): http://creativecommons.org/licenses/by-sa/2.5/deed.en
- Creative Commons Attribution-Share Alike 2.0 Generic (CC-BY-SA 2.0): http://creativecommons.org/licenses/by/2.0/deed.en
- Creative Commons Attribution-Share Alike 1.0 Generic (CC-BY-SA 1.0): http://creativecommons.org/licenses/by-sa/1.0/deed.en
- CC0 1.0 Universal (CC0 1.0) Public Domain Dedication (CC0 1.0) http://creativecommons.org/publicdomain/zero/1.0/deed.en
- GNU Free Documentation License (GFDL): http://en.wikipedia.org/wiki/Wikipedia:Text_of_the_GNU_Free_Documentation_License
- License Art Libre (Free Art License): http://artlibre.org

Timespinner
Press

"June," from the *Brevarium Grimani* by Simon Bening (c.1510)

Other Books from Timespinner Press

The Story of a Special Day

Michael Dobson

A series of (eventually) 366 volumes covering everything that happened on your special day! Events, births, deaths, quotes, holidays, and much more. It's like a birthday card they'll never throw away!

US$7.95 print / US$2.99 ebook.

From Plassey to Pakistan

Humayun Mirza

The history of British Colonial India and the formation of Pakistan from the unique perspective of the son of Pakistan's first president and last of the royal line of Bengal, Bihar, and Orissa! This unique historical document tells the inside story of this distinguished family, including the detailed story of the coup that toppled his father from power!

US$27.95 print

A Whole New Navy: America's War in the Pacific

Miles Durr

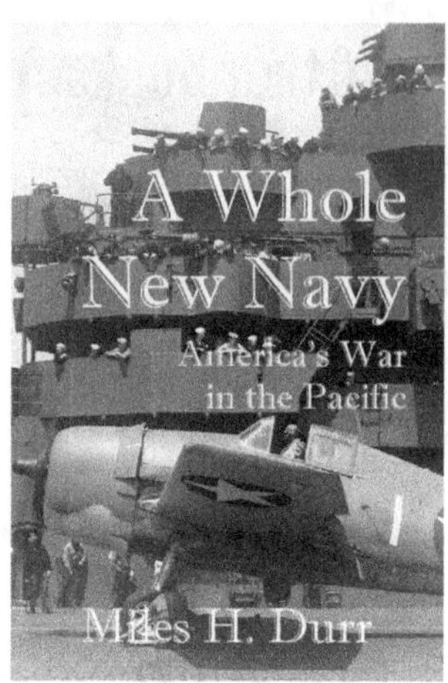

The most comprehensive and detailed description of America's naval war in the Pacific ever—every battle, every ship, every task force and every task group from Pearl Harbor through the Japanese surrender! A must-have for the collection of every World War II buff!

US$29.95 print

Improbable History: The Weird, the Obscure, and the Strangely Important

edited by Michael Dobson

From the birth of Western civilization to the rescue of Apollo 13, from the Leaning Tower of Pisa to Florence's Duomo, history has often turned on small, improbable details. Whatever happened to the ancient Samaritan people? Why did a fortuitous rainstorm allow the British to conquer India? How did an air raid in Italy lead to the development of chemotherapy? What happened when Albert Einstein met Adolf Hitler on the streets of Berlin? How did the Japanese manage to attack the US mainland using balloons? A cast of award-winning writers tackle some of the strangest tales in history!

US$19.95 print

The Letters of William Philip Schwartz 1842-1855

edited by John F. Schwartz

The 19th century soldier and adventurer William Philip Schwartz wrote a series of vivid and detailed letters chronicling his adventures in the Indian Wars, the Mexican-American War, the Gold Rush, and his term as Marine sergeant aboard the USS Constellation. A pioneer in photography, he took *the first known war photographs*. An unforgettable first-hand look into life in the 19th century!

US$17.95 print

Timespinner
Press

www.timespinnerpress.com

June, by Hans Thoma